FINANCIAL LITERACY IN SCHOOLS

DR DHEERAJ MEHROTRA

Copyright © Dr Dheeraj Mehrotra
All Rights Reserved.

Contents

Preface   *v*

1. Importance Of Financial Literacy Among Kids   1

2. Why Financial Literacy In Schools?   18

3. Nep Guidelines   25

4. School Curriculum On Financial Literacy   34

5. A Sample Lesson Plan On Financial Literacy   53

6. The Effective Classroom Practices   71

7. References   79

About The Author   81

Books By The Same Author   85

Preface

Financial Literacy in Schools is an opportunity for the future generation to explore the best of learning and creativity. In today's world, financial literacy is considered as important as basic literacy, i.e., the ability to read and write. Without it, individuals and societies cannot reach their full potential.

The book, Financial Literacy in Schools, is a progressive format per the guidelines of the National Education Policy and aims at paging learning at ease for the students and other stakeholders of the learning community.

Happy Learning!

authordheerajmehrotra.com

IMPORTANCE OF FINANCIAL LITERACY AMONG KIDS

Friends, We know theories related to money, but not the application. We know calculations, but now how to make decisions in money matters. The lack of financial literacy is a global problem, not only for kids but also for adults. (On average, only 30% of the population is financially literate). The reality is that Most of us end up turning to friends and family for financial tips. Many of us do not even know anyone who knows finance. What should we do? The answer is "Start from young and the innocent!". Make financial literacy from the level of A to Z in schools.

Why is financial literacy necessary for children?

Most parents give a piggy bank to their children in which they save their spare change, birthday money or cash gifts received from their relatives/ families. This concept helps them to maintain a discipline of saving. But financial markets are complex and are much beyond the idea of saving only. If children understand the concept of financial markets their age, this can prevent them from later investing in the wrong financial instruments.

When children are aware of the concept, they can influence their families by sharing the knowledge on the importance of savings and taking necessary steps to manage their money better. Thus, spreading the concept of financial literacy and creating economic awareness among children can be a great help.

Teaching Kids about Credit and Debit is the first of its pace toward literacy. We often tell them when and why to use credit and debit cards. Financial Education can affect a better understanding of life and skills. It can give youngsters the information, abilities and certainty to assume responsibility for their lives and construct a safer future for themselves and their families. It is a requisite to teach our kids about SAVINGS. The onset of the global pandemic in 2020 further reinforced the need for financial literacy education for kids, especially at the school level. Many lost jobs and found themselves financially unprepared to handle that unforeseen circumstance. As this topic becomes more mainstream in classrooms, it is hoped that awareness like this will become a valuable resource for educators.

This learning encapsulates freedom and confidence with a better understanding of expenses and earnings. It enables us to the most proficient method to contribute and make riches. For the most part, being monetarily proficient illuminates us in different ways

through which we can put away our cash and create more abundance. It keeps us from going with poor monetary choices. As a matter of fact, and to the priority at large, the young level of financial literacy and youth economic proficiency is frequently underestimated. Besides budgeting, borrowing is another concept that should be included in your child's financial knowledge. Try to explain to them about credit reports, credit scores and what is required to get and maintain a positive credit score. Besides budgeting, borrowing is another concept that should be included in your child's financial knowledge.

Financial schooling should be a constant interaction from youth to adulthood. Sadly, not even our learning organizations appear to perceive this reality. We will quite often accept that individuals will, in some way or another find out about cash all alone. There should be a change in perspective concerning financial education.

Financial literacy or information about how to earn and spend shares that, Indeed, the significance of monetary proficiency for our childhood can't be overemphasized. There's nothing essentially as risky as a monetarily unskilled youth. Somebody who doesn't have a thought on the most proficient method to deal with their funds can undoubtedly fall into different monetary snares accidentally.

It is by and large hard to fix awful choices concerning funds - it can require quite a long while to do as such. Showing youngsters cash early will give them essential information and abilities to help them settle on informed choices about monetary issues. It is essential to expose kids to money and intelligent financial decision-making at a young age. Financial education can make a difference.

The more data you have about funds, the better prepared you will be. Then again, an absence of legitimate information and data about cash is hazardous for any youngster.

For what reason do we go to class to learn about science, math, history and different subjects? The response is to enable us in those separate regions. Essentially, instruction about cash ought to be given similar needs as other disciplines. Youngsters should be engaged with money and how it functions.

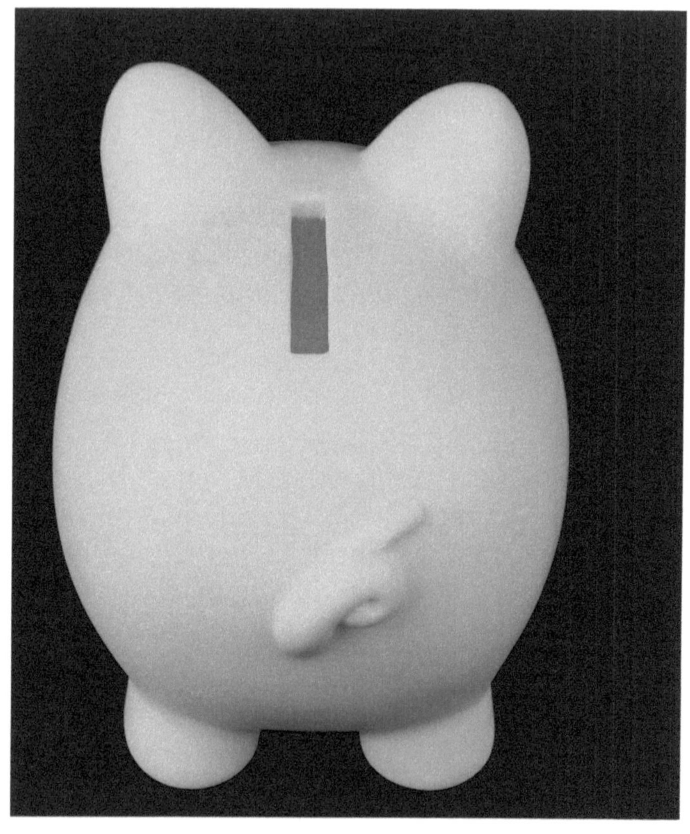

Frequently, youngsters engaged with unfortunate cash propensities; for example, betting had no or unfortunate foundations in financial education. They can be effectively affected by others to participate in other poor monetary dispositions. An individual with a legitimate economic foundation will not be

quickly tricked into partaking in exercises, for example, betting and Ponzi plans.

Here and there, we are up to speed in earnest circumstances that require a lot of cash. For a monetarily proficient youngster, it turns somewhat simpler to move and emerge from the possibility contrasted with a monetarily unskilled.

There are various reasons why financial education is significant for our childhood. They ought to continually be shown how to save, contribute, spending plan and oversee obligations. Inability to do so can prompt an age that is flippant and poor. Youngsters gain tons of practical knowledge as far as they tell - it's called social learning. Generally, kids are shown different subjects like science and math. Notwithstanding, an issue like cash is seldom offered in standard classes or the overall educational plan.

The objective of including Financial Literacy is to make informed financial decisions for the kids as they move into adulthood. Also, teaching personal finance at school is an excellent way to improve the financial capacity of today's young people. The economic attitudes, habits and norms begin to mould *between age 6 and 12 when the student typically is in 1ˢᵗ through 6ᵗʰ grade. Henceforth, teaching children about financial responsibility at those ages can have a long-lasting impact. In the process, financial education can make a difference, and it is imperative to expose kids to money and intelligent financial decision-making to promote financial literacy.*

While the schools tend to teach financial education skills to young learners, many public schools do not include such classes in their curricula. Unfortunately, many children will not have access to crucial financial education. The observations reveal that nearly 2/3ʳᵈ of

Americans cannot pass the basic financial literacy test as per the records observations. In addition, many schools even do not tend to think about being creative. They do not see the topic of Financial Literacy as necessary enough, even though it should be offered just like other classes such as music and art. Also, not all teachers feel confident in teaching personal finance yet due to the specialized and complex nature of many of the topics.

As an essential resource to deliver, the schools must be committed to ensuring that every child has equitable access to a fundamental life skill related to their life's financial outcomes. The schools also need to empower children with the financial abilities and the tools they need to help build a more secure future for themselves and their families. In addition, the schools need to offer financial literacy classes to help kids with their lot.

The research reveals that the curriculum ideally must include personal finance classes for all student age groups from an early age. Also, all elementary school students have to have access to the kid finance class in which the young learners are introduced to the fundamentals of financial literacy; as they enter middle school, students can take the middle school financial literacy class and can explore more advanced topics about budgeting, spending, saving and financial planning.

As with the march of time, the students gain the knowledge needed to manage their financial resources effectively. Finally, in high school, students can take the high school personal finance class, which instils them with practical knowledge on topics such as money management, banking, investing, borrowing, earning power, financial services, insurance stocks and much more.

The idea is to help them make smart financial decisions at all stages of their life. The schools need to enrol the students broadly via remote learning in addition to the dance schools kids, or even coding or other education enrichment programs to give the children the edge they deserve and invest in the future. The plan can be a part of the skill development projects or ongoing experiential learning assignments integrated with other subjects, as financial learning can go along with any issue engaging in financial transactions.

Modern parents look over actually towards teaching kids about money. They also look at what makes the difference between somebody who will eventually become rich and successful in someone who won't so today.

The requirement is towards the awareness of the assets and the liabilities. It is now how simple we make it to clear their concepts. The inclusion must match the basic concepts of building financial independence and understanding the difference between assets and liabilities.

The storytelling should involve incidences like if we have two people making 50000 per month, but they have very defence spending parents. The first one gets the credit card bills and enjoys his money going out shopping, getting the newest phone and the latest TV, indulging and their finest restaurants, getting a new car, a lovely house and all of that nice stuff they typically spend their money on things that make him look good in life. Still, they come back home with credits and bills in a lot of debt. This is wrong and should not be practised.

Teaching them how to manage their money is again of importance. This is a perfect way as many parents to teach their kids about money.

Teaching about living expenses gives the children experience managing money from an early age. This can help when they grow older and they have to work their own money. This is a big contrast to many parents with a poor mentality. The majority of parents rarely talk about money, especially their income. Maintaining a financial diary and planning the monthly budget is always good.

The kids need to be informed about decisions over petty issues. Mentoring them on planning and acquiring the teaching program likewise includes showing kids how to financial plan and get cash. For instance, give kids a financial plan showing the amount you will spend on specific things for themselves and allow them to choose if they would need to utilize their cash to buy the items.

Other than planning, acquiring is one more idea that should be remembered for your youngster's financial information. Attempt to make sense of them about credit reports, FICO ratings and what is expected to get and keep a positive economic assessment. Other than planning, acquiring is one more idea that should be remembered for the youngster's financial information.

Why Financial Literacy in Schools?

The main illustration you should begin showing your kid is the worth of cash. You can do this by giving instances of things and how much value they are about money. For example, you can let them know about a toothbrush and the amount it is sold. You can likewise let them know what a PC is utilized for and the amount it costs.

Students' Financial Literacy (SFL) begins by clearing up for youngsters how cash is acquired. During their initial years, youngsters frequently get money in types of Diwali Greeting Cards, birthday cards or recompense. Nonetheless, you must tell kids that money doesn't come without any problem at that specific time. It should be acquired. Financial education is equally important as other subjects taught in school. Most of us are unaware of many financial issues like card payment, taxes, etc which are the main aspects that are to be dealt with in adulthood

Showing your children how to bring in cash is a significant move toward the course of early monetary training. A primary method for delivering this illustration is by giving them random temp jobs and paying them from there on. These errands ought not to be everyday family tasks but occupations that would typically be finished by somebody you'd normally employ, for example, trimming the grass or washing a vehicle.

Most children grow up without knowing how to save and contribute basically because their folks won't ever do. Be that as it may, sorting your children out for monetary accomplishment by appearing and empowering them to set aside cash for some time later is significant.

A decent approach to doing this is by advising them to save a specific level of any cash they procure constantly. You can make it considerably more tomfoolery by permitting them to enhance reserve funds compartments marked "spend," "save," and "give". Make a

move to recognize saving and financial planning.

Some Requisites showcased as follows:

- *Show your children how to save and contribute.*

-

Most children grow up without knowing how to save and contribute because their folks won't ever do. In any case, setting your children up for monetary accomplishment by appearing and empowering them to set aside cash for some time later is significant. Understanding the term FINANCIAL FREEDOM should be a priority for all students.

•

A decent approach is advising them to continuously save a specific level of any cash they procure. You can make it considerably more tomfoolery by permitting them to enhance reserve funds holders named "spend," "save," and "give". Make a move to recognize saving and effective money management.

Academic qualifications are necessary, and so is financial education. They're both essential, and the schools forget one of them."

- Robert Kiyosaki

Mariam Khan rightly shares that in the cloud,

In the words of the author of "Rich Dad Poor Dad," Financial literacy has long since taken a backseat in a curriculum determined on mining monotonous robots who lack the sense of essential financial management. To the youth currently either entering or preparing to enter the stage of financial independence, high-paying jobs become the penultimate destination.

What one forgets is that it leads to a false sense of financial security as the money they earn is simply ill-spent, in most cases acting as two-way traffic. To explain in simpler words, the capital, instead of being utilised, is spent all together, leaving the person with an empty pocket despite the hours put in the hard work.

Money saved is money earned, but money invested is money profited upon. Though associated with the investment, financial risks may be avoidable if a person is financially intelligent. Research before investment, proper investment and utilisation of assets are some of the fundamental pillars of financial literacy.

Well, the best way to manage your finances is first to become financially literate.

As per Cerebro Kids, which talks about making kids future-ready, Research shows that kids who learn to manage money when they're young will be able to handle their finances as adults better. In real-life situations, students are asked to make decisions where none of the choices is wrong. This helps students in developing decision-making capabilities, as well as becoming prudent in their money-related decision-making. Students about savings, interest, loans, and investments to make them aware of how to handle hard-earned money. In addition, Financial Knowledge and Monetary schooling for youngsters are significant because we need to give them great data and preferred life over ours. Since cash and funds surround us in a more "undetectable" state, we should likewise show their money in various ways. Showing kids cash matters is pretty much as significant as showing them other customary scholarly subjects.

CHAPTER THREE

NEP GUIDELINES

According to: V.L. Ramakrishnan (Ramki), Founder and CEO Shiksha Finance,

After a three-decade-long wait, the National Education Policy (NEP) 2020 was a welcome change for the Indian education sector. The NEP is a set of policies formulated by the Government of India to guide the development of the education sector and promote quality education for its citizens. The first education policy was introduced in 1968, and a second was formulated in 1986, which was subsequently revised in 1992. The 2020 policies aim to transform education in the country and equip students with the right tools to enter the dynamic and technologically advanced workplace. These policies are India's step towards the United Nations Sustainable Goal 4: Quality Education.

There is no better investment towards a society's future than the high-quality education of the youth. Rightly so, the new policy commits to significantly raising educational investment. The Centre and the States will work together to increase the public investment in the education sector to reach 6% of GDP from around 4% of GDP.

Financial support will be provided to various critical components of education and decent service conditions at schools will be ensured so that teachers and students are comfortable and inspired to teach and learn in their schools.

Adequate and safe infrastructure, computing devices, internet, libraries, and sports and recreational resources will be provided to all schools to ensure that teachers and students have a safe, inclusive, and effective learning environment.

Inclusion for children of all genders and children with disabilities will be a priority. NEP 2020 has introduced the "Gender Inclusion Fund" and "Special Education Zones" to build the nation's capacity to provide equitable quality education for all girls and transgender students, differently abled students and students from disadvantaged socio-economic groups. The Fund will help improve access to sanitation and toilets, bicycles and conditional cash transfers. It will also provide unique hostels in dedicated regions, bridge courses, and financial assistance through fee waivers and scholarships.

There is an impending need to improve Gross Enrolment Ratio (GER). The GER is a measure used in the education sector to determine the number of students enrolled in school at several different grade levels Many states and districts of India, like Bihar (13.6%), West Bengal (19.3%), and Jharkhand (19.1%), have a GER below the national average of 25%. The Higher Education Finance Corporation can grant long-term loans to bring the GER of these districts and states to the national average of 10 years. The NEP 2020 focuses on increasing the national GER to 50% by 2023.

The Government's National Scholarship Portal (NSP) can be modelled as a Public-Private-Partnership, with a private-sector board to oversee the organisation. 50% of the funding can be raised from citizens all over India on a 100% tax exemption, with the government putting in 50% of the total.

Innovative devices such as social impact bonds present an exciting alternative by which purpose-driven investors can focus on impact delivery, even if it generates lower returns than a purely commercial investment would.

As education shifts to digital mediums, schools, colleges and institutes will increasingly require financing to improve their digital infrastructure. In recent years, many NBFCs and private financing companies apart from banks have emerged to offer fund Infrastructure loans for schools, colleges and institutes providing vocational and professional courses.

The cost of higher education is increasing gradually, and aspirants search for good options to avail of education loans. These students serve as an attractive target market for financial services providers. Financial service companies have the opportunity to collaborate with the National Scholarship Portal to support students receiving scholarships. These companies can also partner with educational institutions to offer loans and financial support to the students enrolled in such institutions. Increased focus on vocational education in NEP 2020 would also result in the need for financing such vocational courses. The increased technology adoption that the NEP 2020 would bring about *in areas of online learning, e-program delivery, teacher training or e-assessments will serve as a challenge for low-income students in terms of affordability, access to devices and the internet. Such students would require financing not only for their tuition fees but also for the necessary equipment and supplies for their education.*

In a country like ours, where the scale of requirements is this large, such partnerships can support purpose-driven institutions and help transform the education system.

According to the NPCI COO, Praveena Rai, "As the nation develops into an intelligent economy, insight into these crucial topics in the early days of students' formal education will help them expand their horizons. We are confident that the financial literacy textbook will help tender minds absorb basic and advanced financial concepts easily and will establish mindful financial conduct and sound decisions for future generations.

According to the Former CBSE Chairman, Manoj Ahuja, "As the new education policy emphasises the need of nurturing a digital mindset among the students, the books act as a first step towards addressing the same. It focuses on the overall digital payment system, which is new; this small module on financial literacy will educate our students on finance from an early age. The books act interdisciplinary and also stress the growth of money. They refer to skills root and also to the barter system. Adding these books to the curriculum emphasises interdisciplinary development, which even the new education policy confuses.

As per the reports in the economic times, Financial Literacy like every other life skill is crucial. It is always good to expose it to the children in order to instil the money management practice with concepts of saving, spending and investing as a priorities in life. This learning of how to manage money and spend wisely shall help the students to master their goals. For this reason, the schools need to given the opportunities to buy food from the school canteen on and off to keep a check on their spending habits and saving. In addition, the children can be told to have piggy banks for managing saving as a habit.

CHAPTER FOUR

SCHOOL CURRICULUM ON FINANCIAL LITERACY

The ABCs of Wealth curriculum can be implemented in any micro economy worldwide. Generic lesson plans are independent of any local economy.

In addition, CBSE has taken an initiative to sensitize teachers across the country on the basics of Financial Literacy and using relevant Digital Tools in the current scenario. The sessions are being organised regularly to focus will be to create awareness about essential financial planning, how to avoid falling prey to phishing and cyber frauds, etc. This will help educators stay updated to plan their future in a better way. These initiatives are part of Activities related to the Investor Education and Awareness Initiative in terms of SEBI (Mutual Funds) Regulations, 1996.

The primary Level program is appropriate for all ages, emphasising children and youth and concentrating on developing habits and muscles.

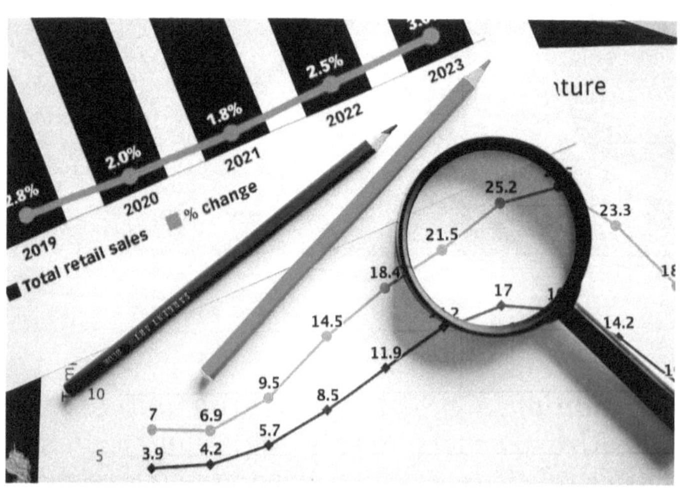

The advanced Level program is appropriate for ages 16 and up and includes various elements of banking services, credit, earning & taxes, retirement, and investing. Our financial literacy curriculum teaches attendees to build a solid foundation in saving, investing, sharing, and spending by developing essential habits and muscles. This development is complemented by learning the goal setting, consultative decision making, borrowing, and

budgeting processes. Furthermore, attendees learn the value and concept of WEALTH and various elements of local financial services. While participants attain the necessary understanding of economic systems during workshops, they are mentored to work as teams within their family and community structure to implement and practice this knowledge in their daily financial lives and those around them.

Finally, show your kids that cash isn't all that matters. This is quite possibly the leading example of monetary schooling for your kids. Sometimes we get so fixated on money to a degree of loving it.

Notwithstanding, you ought to make your kids comprehend that cash is only an instrument for buying. Stress that there are more important things than cash, like loved ones. They ought to know that having cash is significant. However, it isn't all that matters.

As a general rule, monetary instruction is vital to our children. Sadly, guardians frequently will generally expect these straightforward illustrations and careless representations of things to come as the result of not educating them. It is crucial to impart these significant examples to your kids while they are as yet youthful. Teaching about the DIGITAL formats of payments being done and practised by the students in large numbers comes here as a priority.

Including this connects as one of the country's quality-oriented, ease of payment systems.

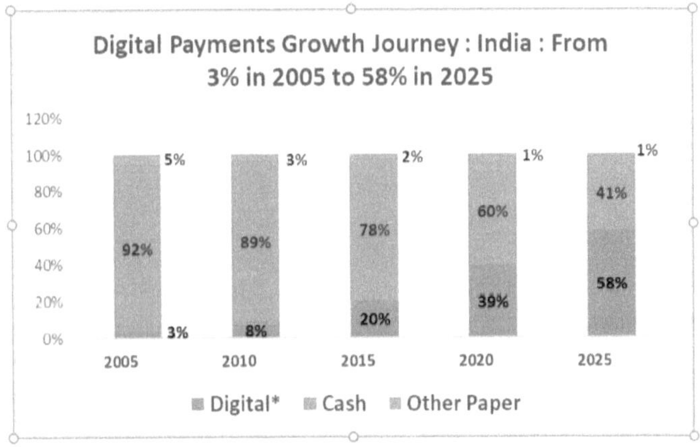

Digital Payments include cards, mobile-based, QR based, wallet-based, and all other electronic modes of payments.

The National Payments Corporation of India (NPCI) and the Central Board of Secondary Education (CBSE) have joined hands to introduce a financial literacy curriculum for students of Class VI. The financial literacy textbook (FLT) is launched as a part of a new elective 'financial literacy' subject that will enable students to understand basic financial concepts at a preliminary stage of their education. The textbook covers crucial topics about financial awareness: starting from teamwork and basic economic concepts to Banking, Security, and modes of Digital Payments such as UPI, Cards, Wallets and more. It entails the origin of banking, the transaction from coins to paper money, types of banks and primary operations and services carried out by banks. The textbook also elucidates the significant role of RBI and the Central government in providing an impetus to the Digital Payments movement.

From core concepts like currency, banking, savings, and investments to advanced concepts like IMPS, UPI, USSD, NACH, PoS, mPoS, QR codes and ATMs, this book cover all that a child might find very useful in a later stage in their life. Building upon the context of modes of digital payments, the book elaborates on the role of UIDAI and the importance of Aadhaar and the Aadhaar Enabled Payment System (AePS). The ABCs of Wealth financial literacy program focuses on helping participants develop various habits. Therefore, workshop learning must be practised at home and in the community environment. In this context, although not required, it would be best if participants could receive an allowance (from parents or guardians) or generate their income regularly (the amount is not necessary at all). Every lesson in the Basic Level includes a take-home handout that allows participants to share their learning with family and community members.

Learning Objective:

Financial literacy helps people in becoming independent and self-sufficient. It gives you basic knowledge of investment options, financial markets, capital budgeting, etc. Understanding your money mitigates the danger of facing a fraud-like situation.

As per the CBSE guidelines,

TOPICS TO BE COVERED:

Teamwork: Learn How to shine with 21st-century skills.

Introduction to financial literacy :

Understanding basic economic concepts,

Barter system, Needs & Wants, Trade, Bill / Cash memo, Need & source of borrowing Banking:

Evolution of Money, Types of Bank, How to open a Bank Accounts, Banking operations.

Security: Role of RBI, Do's & Don'ts for Online Banking

Important Topics such as Awareness may include:

Meaning of Borrowing

Need of Borrowing

Sources of Borrowing

Meaning of Loan

Definition of Central Bank or RBI (Reserve Bank of India)

Functions of RBI

Meaning of Consumer Awareness

Rights of Consumers

Duties of a Consumer

Meaning of a Bank

Concept of Deposits and Loans

Parts of Debit Card and Credit Card

Use of Cheque

Working of Automated Teller Machine

Opening a Bank Account

Features of Saving Bank Account

Features of Current Account

Meaning of Recurring Deposits

Meaning of Fixed Deposits

E-Banking

Real Time Gross Settlement (RTGS)

National Electronic Funds Transfer (NEFT)

In addition, some short-term programmes can be floated with content as follows:

Topics to be covered :

1. Evolution of Money
2. Metaverse
3. Cryptocurrency & NFT
4. Savings, Budgeting & Smart Spending
5. Decision-Making Framework

The private players are rushing to explore this notion within schools. FinSmart program ensures that children understand and interact with money with a bold, brave, brilliant attitude and awareness.

Financial wisdom inculcates confidence, street-smartness, and a healthy risk attitude in life. Finkeyz FinSmart curriculum is designed by Goldman Sachs, National Payments Corporation of India (NPCI) and alumni of IIM Ahmedabad and IIM Calcutta.

In addition, a term like FINANCIAL PLANNING has to be rooted in every lesson to understand the concepts. Financial planning is

not a one-shot thing but a continuous practice that starts with any individual getting her first job.

Marriage, your child's birth, their growing up, even their retirement from work and continues even afterwards. All through the years, one can live an uncompromised life if individuals are mindful of their financial decisions and stay secure from all uncertainties that may come up.

Finance Tips:

When you are young, personal finance tips start earning for the first time as parents and educators.

- *Keep a good credit report. Repay all dues on time and never be on revolving credit*

- *Control Your Spending by cutting costs on things that do not add value to your life*

-

Create an Emergency Fund that can cover at least six months' livelihood and ensure financial security during hard times.

Managing finances and budgeting tips when you are a newly married couple

- *Establish a budget, live within your means and prioritize basic needs*

- *Open two joint savings accounts. One for emergency savings and the other one to cover luxuries and sudden expenses*

- *Invest a portion of your income, get life and health cover and grow your money through more investment options like stocks, commodities, mutual funds, and cryptocurrencies.*

Smart and right investment tips when you are a new parent:

-

Include the newborn in your existing health insurance policy within 30 or 60 days post-delivery

- *Update your family budget and start investing in tax-saving instruments like home loans and children's education plans to lower your taxable income*

- *Start saving for your child's education to create a sizeable fund for school, college and higher study expenses.*

Money-saving tips before and after retirement when you are a senior citizen

- *Plan for retirement while you are still working to maintain the same standard of living even after you have stopped working*

- *Open new revenue streams by renting out our house to tenants, taking up part-time jobs as a coach, consultant, or even an artist in case you have creative hobbies.*

-

Leverage the senior citizen benefits on rail or flights and invest in guaranteed income schemes like bank Fixed Deposits and government bonds.

52

Source: https://t2.reminders.hdfclife.com/webApp/ COL_Financial_Planning_090822_LP

CHAPTER FIVE

A SAMPLE LESSON PLAN ON FINANCIAL LITERACY

Pricing & Rounding:

Gathering together is significant cash expertise for youngsters to acquire before they are liable for their funds. Assuming that a sticker price says Rs. 125.99, understudies ought to perceive that because the number beginnings with a one don't mean the cost is near that sum. Mark things in the class with prices understudies need to gather together and plan.

Class Store:

This activity is an excellent student guide to start understanding item pricing and begin to learn about amounts and the worth of items. To build your classroom store, grab pencils, posters, your computer, and the projector (things of different values) and ask your students to guess the prices before you mark them yourself.

Money Sorting Math:

This educational game is easy and can be added or adapted to make it more challenging for older learners. Put a variety of coins in a jar and have your students sort them by value. Next, write different amounts on the board and ask them to produce the correct parts. Explain how the same amount can be achieved using different coin combinations. Explain PRICE as a financial term. Eg. I paid a heavy Price for this product—concepts of Selling Price and Cost Price. Explain terms like SALE. What it talks about is 50% Sale etc.

In addition, the term Transaction is also essential to understand—the difference between TRANSACTION and SALE. The transaction is a process, and SALE is an activity.

Concepts of GAIN and PROFIT. Loss and Profit.

Coin Searching Dough

Sensory activities are a great way to spice up a more serious subject. Make basic cloud dough with flour and baby oil and hide some coins. Have your kiddos feel and squeeze around to find the cash and count them afterwards.

Play Grocery Market

Create your classroom supermarket or a KIRANA SHOP, and have each student bring a grocery item or any commodity to class. Have different shelves labelled according to the type of item and price? Ask your students to sort all the things and talk about budgets and sales for a better knowledge of saving.

Roll and Count Game

Get some dice and a bunch of different coins. Gather your students around and have them take turns rolling the dice and collecting the coin amount for the combined numbers they rolled. 2-3 dice are suitable for this; coins of minor amount act as a ready reckoned to this. This teaches them about CURRENCY—the concept of BANK.

WHEN YOU SUPPORT
A SMALL BUSINESS,
YOU'RE SUPPORTING
A DREAM.

Forms of Currency:

INR- Indian Rupees

61

USD- US Dollars

POUND- British Pound

YEN- Japanese

Australian Dollars

Canadian Dollars

FINANCIAL VOCABULARY FOR KIDS

Some of the words which require sharing among the kids as a FINANCIAL Vocabulary include as follows:

1. Interest Rate

2. Investment

3. External capital

4. Cash outflow

5. Revenue

6. Profit

7. Loss

8. Recession

9. *Debt*

10. *Collateral*

11. *Mortgage*

12. *Short-term loan*

13. *Long-term loan*

14. *Credit rating*

15. *Overdraft*

16. *Shares*

17. *Stocks*

18. *Rally*

19. *Bull market*

20. *Bear market*

21. *Break Even Point*

22. *Sale*

23. *Discount*

24. *Transaction*

25. *Offer Price*

26. *Sale Price*

27. *GDP*

28. *Loss*

29. *Books of Account*

30. *Liabilities*

31. *Gross*

32. *Assets*

33. *Salary*

34. *Gross*

35. *Net*

36. *Financial Planning*

Essential learning about SAVINGS, Needs Vs Wants, and Emergency Fund.

What Is Savings?

Learning to save is foundational for managing money well and building wealth. This is a basic money concept that students at all levels can grasp. The familiar "piggy bank" imagery helps kids to make the association and quickly get the message of the poster.

What Are Needs. Vs. Wants?

Distinguishing between something you need and something you want is another essential concept in financial literacy that is relevant and any grade level. This poster sets up a great discussion point on this topic. Teachers can use it to build a conversation and get kids thinking about the concept. Furthermore, it can help to spark a simple game that kids can take home and use with their family in their real life.

A what and why of the above goes a long way in making things clear to them and preparing them for learning for life.

A basic financial vocabulary tutorial stands at

https://www.youtube.com/ watch?v=aQeeX7xyOWI

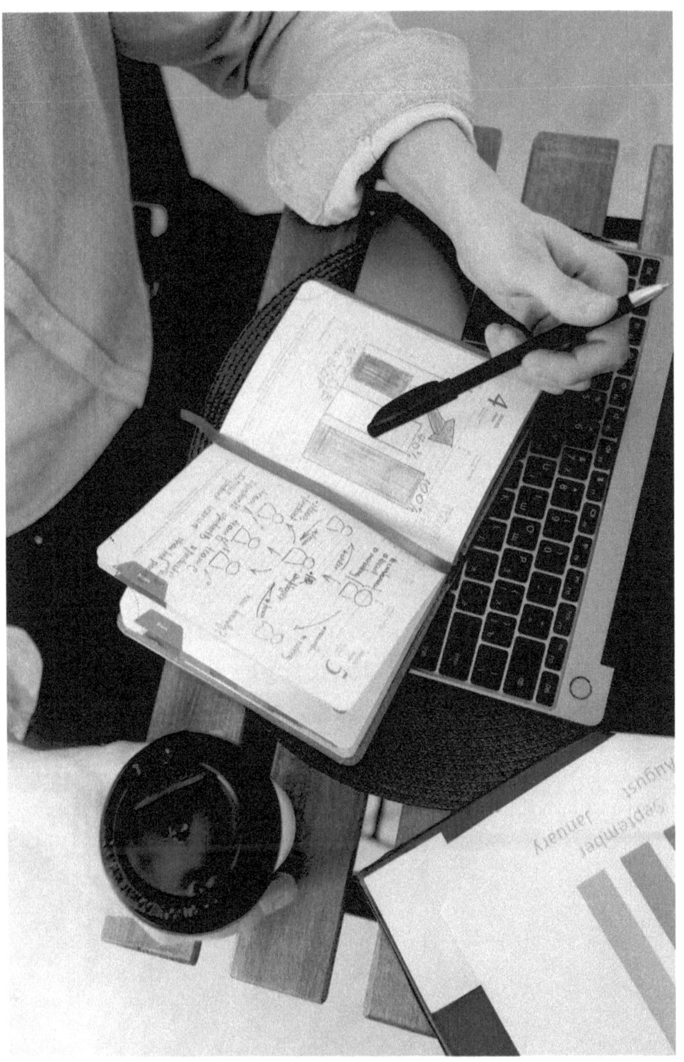

"Invest for the long haul. Don't get too greedy, and don't get too scared." "The best way to

measure your investing success is not by whether you're beating the market but by whether you've put in place a financial plan and a behavioural discipline that are likely to get you where you want to go."

"The stock market is a device to transfer money from the impatient to the patient."

Warren Buffett

"The intelligent investor is a realist who sells to optimists and buys from pessimists."

Benjamin Graham

CHAPTER SIX

THE EFFECTIVE CLASSROOM PRACTICES

The best chance to permit students to learn about your arrangements is through the whole first day. Likewise, before courses start, you would unquestionably have to comprehend what to expect from students and precisely how

they can fulfil those suppositions. Thus, while discussing the class approaches on the first day, verify that they remember it and perceive the impacts of not adhering to the rules. Assuming you miss the mark to depict or offer punishments or repercussions for penetrating class rules, students would be sure not to follow them on the whole.

The students that frequently come to be unruly are squeezed directly into violent ways of behaving because they are worn out. It is ideal to forestall an extended talk. Assuming that you stay to do that, your students would positively rest or play around with their PDAs and different thingamajigs. Thinking you see that it would unquestionably take a tactical preceding, your students can keep being lashed in their seats inside the accompanying hour and incorporate different kinds of errands after that.

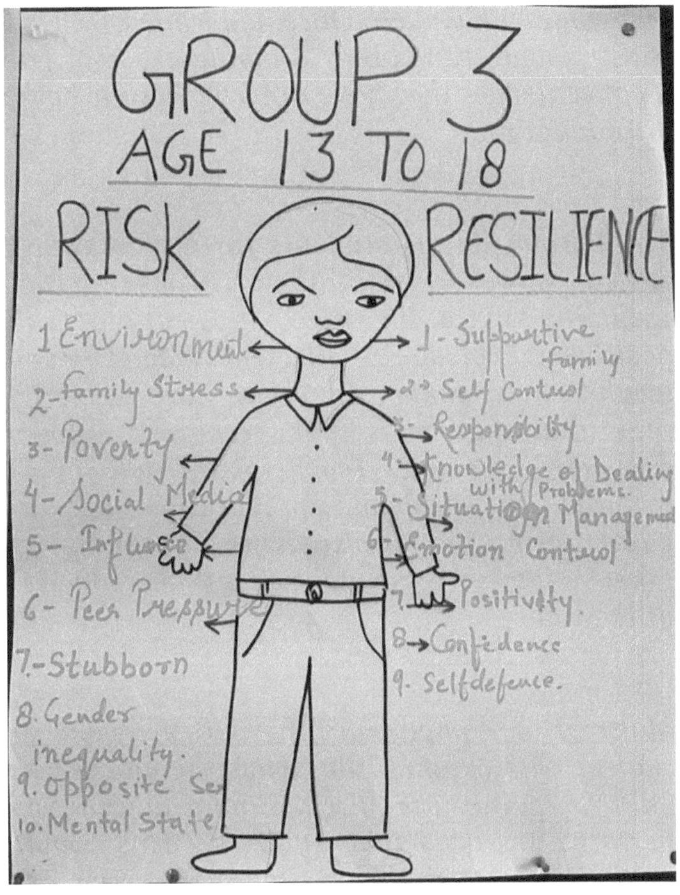

A *different technique that teachers use is causing their learners truly to feel that they genuinely deal with them. You can ask precisely how they are at the point you see them. If they are genuinely boisterous, you could draw them*

out when each individual is dynamic and ask him what is mistaken. Once in a while, students will unquestionably illuminate a few inconveniences they have run over in your home or foundation.

The bottom line is students furthermore have stifled power inside them. Those power assuming extra in their illustrations will positively explode in different means. As a teacher, you would ultimately have to verify that that power is put resources into a supportive method. Teachers are not simply inspired by academic preparation but by guaranteeing that the students' capacities are taken into tremendous and productive utilization.

Make it a component of your program or subject curriculum. Talk about the guidelines, point-by-point, if required. Similar to what you perform in academic subjects. This would undoubtedly aid clean out any type of misconception and also incorrect analysis.

For the majority of educators, they would undoubtedly have three tasks in a forty-five min duration. The pupil reach launches their power and also, at the same time, find out something. Suppose your students attempt to depart the conversation right into something unnecessary; after that, do not claim that directly. You can try to attach it and afterwards begin to return to the initial subject if your trainees are coming to be confrontational; after that, do not say to make them concur with you. They will undoubtedly withstand extra if you require them. Allow them to see what the repercussions of their negative behaviour are.

A mentor can be challenging if energetic and also loud trainees will undoubtedly interrupt the lessons. As an educator, maintaining the classes and also rolling conversations can be tricky if you keep obtaining disturbed. This is confirmed to be challenging for those beginning their training career.

If you are having trouble with details pupils and they are coming to be way too much for you to manage, do not require it on your own. Several elements or individuals in the institution's management can assist. You can speak to the assistance counsellor and request suggestions on how to deal with or deal with the problem. If the pupil will undoubtedly coordinate, you can have them satisfy the counsellor themselves.

Class administration describes just how educators see to it that lessons proceed despite the interruption. Class monitoring aids instructors in taking care of concerns regarding inspiration, self-control and regard. Instructors utilise various techniques and strategies to show that their pupils are motivated, inspired, and mannerly. Naturally, methods would undoubtedly depend upon the instructor's choice.

CHAPTER SEVEN

REFERENCES

https://www.teachingexpertise.com/classroom-ideas/financial-literacy-lesson-plans/

https://government.economictimes.indiatimes.com/news/education/cbse-introduces-financial-literacy-booklet-for-students-curated-by-npci/83987904

https://www.highereducationdigest.com/nep-2020-and-the-role-of-education-finance-in-india/

https://mindtreasures.com/financial-literacy/

Source: https://t2.reminders.hdfclife.com/webApp/COL_Financial_Planning_090822_LP

https://www.risevision.com/blog/free-financial-literacy-posters-for-k-12-schools

https://www.financialexpress.com/money/why-financial-literacy-is-important-for-children/2334907/

About The Author

Dheeraj Mehrotra, MS, MPhil, PhD (Education Management) honoris causa., a white and a yellow belt in SIX SIGMA, a Certified NLP Business Diploma holder, is an Educational Innovator, Author, with expertise in Six Sigma In Education, Academic Audits, Neuro-Linguistic Programming (NLP), Total Quality Management In Education, an Experiential Educator, a CBSE Resource towards School Assessment (SQAA), CCE, JIT, Five S, and

KAIZEN. He has authored over 100 books on topics which include Computer Science, AI, Digital Body Language, NLP, Quality Circles, School Management, Classroom Effectiveness and Safety and security in schools. A former Principal at De Indian Public School, New Delhi, (INDIA), NPS International School, Guwahati, and Education Officer at GEMS, Gurgaon, with an ample teaching experience of over Two Decades, he is a certified Trainer for Quality Circles/ TQM in Education and QCI Standards for School Accreditation/ School Audits and Management. He has also been honoured with the President of India's National Teacher Award in the year 2006 and the Best Science Teacher State Award (By the Ministry of Science and Technology, State of UP), Innovation in Education for his inception of Six Sigma In Education by Education Watch, New Delhi and Education World- Best Teacher Award, BOLT Learner Teacher Award by Air India, 'Innovation in Education Award 2016' by Higher Education Forum (HEF), Gujarat Chapter, among others. He has developed over 150 FREE EDUCATIONAL MOBILE Apps for the Google Play Store exclusively for Teachers, Students, and Parents. This work has been recognised by the LIMCA BOOK OF RECORDS & INDIA BOOK OF RECORDS as the only Indian to draw that feast. Dr Mehrotra works as a PRINCIPAL at KUNWARS GLOBAL SCHOOL, Lucknow, in India. He has conducted over 1000 workshops globally on "Excellence In Education" integrated with Total Quality Management and Six Sigma, Technology Integration in Education (TIE), Developing towards being ROCKSTAR TEACHERS, including Cyberspace, Cyber Security, Classroom Management, School Leadership & Management, and Innovative teaching within classrooms via Mind Maps, NLP and Experiential Learning in

Academics. He is an active TEDx speaker and can be viewed on the youtube TEDx channel. As a premium UDEMY Instructor, he has developed over 450 courses and caters to over 8 Lakh students from 180 countries. He can be visited at www.authordheerajmehrotra.com.

Books By The Same Author

A Must For All Home Libraries
Preparing Parenting Mindset For Futuristic Learning
Dr Dheeraj Mehrotra
Paperback: ₹ 99
Available at
flipkart.com
amazon
www.authordheerajmehrotra.com

PRIORITY LEARNING FOR EDUCATORS
It is worth knowing now!
digital body Language
WORK ETHICS FOR TEACHERS
TEACHER'S TOOLKIT POST COVID
TOWARDS EXCELLENCE IN TEACHING & LEARNING
200 WOW TEACHING IDEAS
NLP FOR TEACHERS
Towards Quality Teaching Skills
Teachers' Favourite Teaching Strategies That Work
Buy now at amazon.in
APPLYING SIX SIGMA WITHIN CLASSROOMS
DR. DHEERAJ MEHROTRA
EXPERIENTIAL LEARNING FOR EDUCATORS
TOWARDS QUALITY LITERACY FOR ALL
Academic Audits In Schools
What, Why & How?